The Mountains Still Call

poetry by
Jyn Banta

CHAPTERS

Chapter One
A Call From The Depths

Chapter Two
Above All My Troubles

Chapter Three
Sunlit Trees

Chapter Four
Beyond Everything

"The mountains are calling me
and I must go."
-John Muir

Chapter One

A Call From The Depths

we all have those dark places
deep within our souls
unfilled by light
begging to be explored

i feel that longing
as i step foot
on these mountains
it calls to me
begging to be explored

for all of those people
for whom nature
is a beacon of hope
i hope these words
resonate with you

it felt like a dream.

my name whispered
by the wind herself
flowing through the trees

come.

and so i did.

when i walk
through this forest
it feels as if
i am walking
through the heart
of the universe

i find such eloquence
in the stanzas of the clouds
begetting
elegance upon elegance

nature's peace
flows like sunlight

close your eyes
breathe in

exhale.

feel your problems dissipate
and let in the light.

there is something about
the mountains

that feels
like home.

it is only through
exploration
of nature's boundlessness

that we can explore
our own inner restlessness

human beings
are not machines
dedicated
to taking in instructions
and spitting out money.

we are meant
to touch the stars
and grace the heavens
with our unchained life force.

do not let this world
hold you down onto the earth

no, my love
reach for the stars.
reach for them
while you still can.

the details
in the rings
of a tree
are the fingerprints
of a connected world
one we are meant
to be a part of

i feel such a sense
of loss
when i consider
our detachment from nature

we have made her the enemy
when she is truly our mother.

my spirit breathes in
with the rising sun
and out
as it sets
each cycle of breath
bringing life to my body

there are countless doorways
to hidden places
buried in the mysticism
of the forests

in each of these
we find a piece
of our missing souls

life is short
but that is not a curse
it is a blessing in disguise

our existence is but a flicker
but an ephemeral flame
which exists only
for a small moment
and dissipates to dirt.

there are more lessons
to be learned
about life
in studying
the movement of a bird's wings
than you could ever learn
by sitting in a classroom

your life can be more
than vague disappointment
and dread for the future

great freedom awaits
where nature begins
and humanity ends

we have only one life
and yet most of us
squander it
in front of screens

there is no greater companion
than the self.

as long as we are
good and kind
leaving memories
in the minds of others

we cannot truly die

a bird flaps its wings
spreading poetry
through the air
the likes of which
cannot be replicated
with mere paper and pen

in times of trouble
turn to nature
for wisdom

let it teach you
the strength of lions
the wisdom of eagles
the resilience of mountains
and the flexibility of streams

let nature teach you
and set you free.

let go of the past-
you cannot grow new flowers
until the old ones
have decomposed into soil.

live in the moment
grasping the vitality
of each passing second

Chapter Two

Above All My Troubles

songs of freedom
around the campfire
celebrating life
as the embers fly

power
and wisdom
emanate
from the rivers
and streams

even
the embers
of the brightest of fires
could not glow so brightly
as to outshine your eyes

commune with nature
by meditating
and just existing
in complete peace

the sun rose
over the mountains
and i leaned over
to kiss you

with the subtlest smile
you welcomed
this new adventure

there is no greater freedom
in the world
than the knowledge
that you are complete
as you are
and you need nothing
and no one else
to feel at peace

human power
lies in our ability
to disobey.

subvert authority
push against the system
fight for your right
to be an individual

you make me feel
as if i am dreaming
though i am awake

you make me feel
like i'm touching the stars
though i only lay by your side

you make me feel
as if nothing in the world
could put a stop to our love

and through our love
i am beginning to believe it.

we do not see the irony
in seeking to fill
a broken heart
with more love

we seek healing
at the hand of a sword

change
is not a bad word

the rules of society
are artificial constructs
meant to control us

we must fight back
and break the rules
wherever we find them

society
is a chain
around our necks

to me, you are
a magnifying glass
making ever new feeling
every sensation
every sunrise and sunset

all the more
beautiful.

we waste our lives
chasing after paper
acquiring just enough of it
just in time to die.

this is no way to live.

she put me in a trance
a hypnosis, even
with the way she moved

as a society
we have worshipped money
for far too long
placing it far above
everything else

compassion for the poor
opportunities for everyone

this is what we need.

only when you get lost
can you find yourself

i swear, my love
you are the only one
who understands me

rules were meant
to be broken

this great longing
all of us feel
which we seek to fill
with money, cars, possessions

is merely an innate desire
to be something more
than just a small,
nameless part
in a huge machine.

the powerful
seek to control
our individuality

for they know
that it threatens
conformity

it is such a shame
that we cannot look
through the eyes
of someone else

if we could
i am quite sure
that all of our problems
would fade away

take a walk
in the morning
do not think of anything
or talk to anyone
just let yourself exist
and take in the beauty
of this earth

clothes won't make you happy
money won't make you happy
cars won't make you happy
drugs wont make you happy

the only thing
that can make you happy
is you.

do not merely
trim the branches
of the tree of problems
in your life

go to the root.
look inside yourself
examine your flaws
and do the hard work
to make yourself better.

i would trade
all the city lights
in the world
for one cumulous cloud

love
is a rose
with thorns

admire it from a distance
but do not attempt
to control it
for that is where
pain is inflicted.

Chapter Three

Sunlit Trees

no one has ever
understood anyone
as well as you
understand me

if your life
amounts
to just a collection
of possessions

have you really lived at all?

dance with me
as the sun sets
lets keep going
until the moon rises
and the stars are visible

oh, dance with me
until the world ends.

as long as you have
hope
you have everything you need.

solitude
just means
being comfortable
without others around.

you were born for this moment.

for seizing your opportunity.

you were born to conquer.

this, and so much more.

from the moment we are born
our perfect souls
once a still pond
become polluted lakes
full of all sorts
of terrible advice.

perhaps one must lose
one's mind
in order find
one's soul

life is a glacier
moving slowly
but surely
changing things
not noticeably,
but definitely.

you are the sun
that lights up my mornings

she was not afraid
of new;
new experiences
new people
new loves

she was not afraid
of the dark.

find someone to love
who you wouldn't mind
following
to the ends of the earth
and back.

the song of nature
though we may not hear it
never ends

time spent on self-love
is never a waste;
rather than taking away
from your life
it adds to it.

in that little tent
on the forest floor
under the stars
and covered in moonlight

we did what came naturally
we moved
with the forces of nature

and that is a night
i will never forget.

my love, no photograph
could ever contain
the love we have
for each other.

nature heals the wounds
left in our hearts
by our fellow human beings.

follow me
into some unknown place
let's survive
off of the land
and forget
everything we know
about society
and its rules

i swear, every love song
ever written
must have been written
for you.

the greatest delight
of individuality
is nonconformity.

to imitate others
is to disrespect the person
you were meant
to actually be

take care of your inner light
for it will guide you way
when the night is darkest
and seems most dangerous.

Chapter Four

Beyond Everything

beyond everything
is our inner light
keeping us warm
in the darkest night

each new day
is a fresh opportunity
to begin anew
and leave behind
your old patterns

do not revolve your life
around your problems.

instead, revolve your life
around fulfilling your dreams.

instinct
is the most powerful weapon
human kind can possess

surround yourself
with people
who push you forward
and fill you with light

the ultimate strength of man
is to be the master
of his own desires.

education is a valuable thing
but there are things
that one learns
from a life of adventure
that cannot be taught
in a crusty old textbook.

you can do anything
you want to in life
if only you can conquer
your fears.

ultimately
the only thing
holding you back
is yourself

a good person is one who
wishes to sow joy in the
garden of humanity rather than
sorrow or pain.

for every evil
there is a stronger good
for every darkness
there is a vaster light
for every sorrow
there is boundless happiness

everything has its equal
and its balance.

the truest peace
is found in the wilderness

the darkest of nights
is only an opportunity
for the brightest of lights
to come, triumphant
and make a lesson
of the fact
that life always wins.

sometimes
the most important thing
is just to keep moving
even when it feels
like you can't..

you can.
find the strength
in yourself
and push onward.

no matter what happens
remember that this
is not the end
of your story

you have so much life
left to live
and you will soon forget
the turmoil of the moment.

do not allow your mistakes
to define you.

you are more
than your mistakes.

every darkness will end

i promise you this much.

our success is not defined
by the wealth we amass

it is defined
by the joy
we bring to the lives
of others

there have never been
two hands
as perfectly fitted
to be held by each other
than ours.

humanity is at war with death
when we should instead
be at peace with it

for it is as natural as life
and no evil thing
and should be treated as such.

though you are just
a small part
of the grander puzzle

the puzzle would not
be complete
without you

the greatest thing
you could do
with your life

is to spend it
becoming
who you truly are.

despite every adversity
the river finds its way
across the landscape

in the same way
you will overcome everything
and become the person
you are meant to be

take comfort, for it is only
a matter
of time.

let the ocean erode
everything that is false
about you

let the sands
wear down
your sharpest edges

let life
transform you
from pain into light.

the sun still rises
the birds still sing
the mountains still call
live still goes on

remember this;
all things must end.

ABOUT THE BOOK

"The Mountains Still Call" is a poetry book about finding your calling, discovering your true self, and living a better life through finding peace and empowering yourself.